# Most Popular
# Puerto Rican Recipes
## Quick & Easy

A Cookbook of Essential Food Recipes Direct from Puerto Rico

*By*

Grace Barrington-Shaw

**More books by Grace-Barrington-Shaw:**

## Disclaimer

All reasonable efforts have been made to provide accurate and error-free recipes within this book. These recipes are intended for use by persons possessing the appropriate technical skill, at their own discretion and risk. It is advisable that you take full note of the ingredients before mixing and use substitutes where necessary, to fit your dietary requirements.

# Contents

# Introduction

Puerto Rican cuisine is an intermingling of Latin, Taino, West African, Spanish American and Caribbean cultures. Locally grown and imported ingredients are used to create these dishes which generally offer exceptional flavors but typically also a high caloric content. One thing is sure, the foods you will encounter in Puerto Rico will not soon be forgotten, you'll be delighted by the awesome spread that Puerto Rican cuisine has to offer. Island natives and visitors can attest to the indelible impression Puerto Rican food tends to leave on the mind and also the taste buds. If you have yet to visit Puerto Rico, the recipes in this short book will allow you to experience a sample which may just see you placing your vacation plans in motion to include a visit there.

A distinguishing characteristic of Puerto Rican food is the meatiness and crunchiness of many dishes. Sofrito is a common additive or accompaniment, as well as spicy adobo seasoning that can be used in meat dishes, soups or rice. It is also common for many of the dishes to be accompanied by plantains. This high demand for plantain on the island results in the plantain supply being supplemented with imports.

The beverage of choice for spicy dishes is a cold refreshing beer, whether a Puerto Rican brand or another popular imported beer from the US or Mexico. The most demanded alcoholic beverage however is rum, much of which is local and is consumed straight up or in cocktail mixes. A Spanish tradition which is still common in Puerto Rico is the practice of having a strong cup of black coffee to round off an evening meal.

This book contains a representation of meals: breakfast, lunch/dinner, snack, dessert and beverage options. Enjoy creating these and become introduced to or reacquainted with an authentic Puerto Rican dining experience

# FREE Bonuses

We have 3 **FREE** bonus cookbooks for your enjoyment!

- **Cookie Cookbook** 2134 recipes
- **Cake Cookbook** 2444 recipes
- **Mac and Cheese Cookbook** 103 recipes

Simply visit: **www.ffdrecipes.com** to get your **FREE** recipe ebooks.

You will also receive free exclusive access to our World Recipes Club, giving you FREE best-selling book offers, discounts and recipe ideas, delivered to your inbox regularly.

# 1. Sorullitos de Maiz (Deep Fried Corn Meal Sticks and Dipping Sauce)

These fritters which are also known as Spanish or Latin fritters, have a perfectly crunchy exterior with a soft and sweet centre. You can choose to enjoy them as a snack, lunch or appetizer item and they may also be made with cheese in the middle if you so choose.

Serves 6

**Ingredients**

1 tbsp. butter

2 C. water

1 tsp salt

3 tbsps.granulated sugar

½ C. mayonnaise

1 C. cornmeal

2½ C. vegetable oil

Garlic salt to taste.

¼ C. ketchup

**Preparation**

1. Boil some water in a pot then add sugar, salt, and butter.

2. When dissolved, turn the heat down to a low flame then add a cup of the cornmeal, whisking until smooth.

3. When a dough has been formed, pour all the oil into a deep, frying pan and heat to 350 F.

4. Using oil greased hands, form about three tbsps of the dough into a ball then roll into a long cylinder, not more than three inches long and about half an inch in thickness. Fry about three or four sticks each batch and oil hands as necessary.

5. The sticks are ready when they become golden brown in color. Set to drain on an absorbent paper towel and serve while warm.

6. To make the dipping sauce, combine the mayonnaise, garlic salt and ketchup well and have with sticks.

**Pairs well with** – cheese dip, mayo ketchup

# 2. Carne Guisada III

This popular Puerto Rican dish is present on menus in most homes and restaurants. It is known in some spheres as the perfect dish and when you taste it, you're sure to understand why it is dubbed so.

Serves 4

## Ingredients

8 ounces canned tomato sauce

¼ C. sofrito sauce

1 small packet sazon seasoning

1 tbsp adobo seasoning

½ teaspoon dried oregano

Salt, to taste

2 lbs beef stew

2 C. peeled and cubed potatoes

1 C. water

## Preparation

1. Mix the tomato sauce, sofrito, sazon and adobo seasonings, along with the oregano and salt in a large pot.

2. Simmer the contents on a low to medium flame for about five 5 minutes.

3. Add the meat and allow it to brown evenly then pour in some water until the meat is just covered.

3. Simmer the meat and sauces, cover for an hour, then add the potatoes and cook for another half an hour.

**Pairs well with** – steamed rice

# 3. Horchata de Arroz (Rice Drink)

This delicately cinnamon flavored drink is a refreshing creamy delight. Some people prefer to boil the rice however this particular recipe uses rice that has been soaked overnight, then used as is. Crushed ice can also be used to make a slushy version.

Serves 4

**Ingredients**

1 C. long grain rice, white

½ C. white sugar

3 C. cold water

12 ounces evaporated milk

1 tsp vanilla

½ tsp cinnamon powder

**Preparation**

1. Soak the rice overnight in a bowl of water.

2. Pour the water off the rice after straining through a sieve.

3. Combine the cold water and evaporated milk then blend half of it along with the soaked rice in a blender.

4. After about half a minute of blending, add the cinnamon, sugar and vanilla then continue blending with the other half of the milk mixture added.

5. Double a cheesecloth, place in a strainer, then strain the liquid. The solids can be thrown away. Strain again if needed and serve with ice.

**Pairs well with** – Mallorcas

# 4. Puerto Rican Meat Patties

These deep-fried meat patties are perfect as an appetizer or snack and are made even better with a dip. They are also quite satisfying on their own.

Serves 8

**Ingredients**

3 tbsps. olive oil

1 lb. ground beef

4 minced cloves garlic

1 ½ cups cilantro, chopped

2 qts. vegetable oil to fry patties

1 chopped onion

1 chopped bell pepper, green

7 ½ ounces tomato sauce

1 x 16 oz. egg roll wrapper package

**Preparation**

1. Using a heavy bottom frying pan, put the olive oil to heat up over a medium flame.

2. Add the chopped garlic, onions, peppers and sauté until tender.

3. Add the ground beef and when browned, pour off extra fat and add the tomato sauce and cilantro.

4. When the cilantro has wilted, remove the pan from the heat and allow contents to cool for handling.

5. Spoon about two to three table spoons of the meat into a wrapper and fold it to achieve a triangular shape. Seal the edges with a bit of water. Continue until all the meat has been used up.

6. Put the vegetable oil to heat in a deep frying pan to 360 F.

7. Fry the patties until they are golden brown then soak up any excess oil, place the patties onto absorbent towels.

**Pairs well with**–salsa, guacamole

# 5. Coquito

This national Puerto Rican, traditional drink is popular during the festive season. In fact, the Christmas holidays are incomplete without it!

Serves 8

## Ingredients

4 C. coconut milk

6 tbsps. white sugar

2 tsps. vanilla

½ tsp grated nutmeg

8 tbsps. dark rum

8 eggs, yolks only

## Preparation

1. Mix the coconut milk together with the sugar and scald in a saucepan on a medium flame.

2. Add the vanilla to the egg yolks and beat in half a cup of the coconut sugar mixture.

3. Now pour the egg yolks into the remaining coconut milk in the pot and stir constantly on a low flame. Stop cooking when the mixture reaches 160 F.

4. Do not allow the mixture to boil.

5. Strain the mixture into a container then add the rum. Allow to cool to room temperature.

6. Refrigerate with plastic wrap touching the surface of the liquid until well cold. Sprinkle nutmeg on top to serve.

**Pairs well with** – arroz con gandules, pastels, pernil

# 6. Mallorcas (Puerto Rican Ham and Egg Sandwiches)

These sandwiches are made from freshly baked pan de Mallorca. The bread receives its name from Mallorca in Spain from which the recipe originates. It is fluffy, light, sweet and perfectly balanced with the savory ham and cheese flavors.

Serves 6

**Ingredients**

¼ ounce active dry yeast

½ C. milk

2 ½ C. flour

¼ C. sugar

6 eggs

Powdered sugar, to dust

3 lightly beaten egg yolks

1 teaspoon kosher salt

18 deli ham slices

12 ounces cheddar cheese, sliced

15 tbsps. Melted unsalted butter (add extra to grease pan)

## Preparation

For Rolls

1. Add the yeast to quarter cup water at a temperature of 115 F. Leave for ten minutes until it foams.

2. Combine the milk, quarter of the butter and the egg yolks then add it to the yeast mixture. Mix until smooth.

3. Put in the flour, sugar, and the salt then stir until the dough is formed. Turn out onto a counter or suitable surface and knead till smooth.

4. Place in greased bowl, cover with cling wrap and leave until it doubles its size.

5. Turn out onto floured counter then roll out into a rectangle (about 18 x 18 inches).

6. Use two table spoons of butter to brush the surface then tightly roll from short end to short end as you would a cinnamon roll.

7. Slice into 6 even pieces then place flat side down onto a greased rectangular baking tray.

8. Cover once more with cling wrap and allow to double. Bake in oven preheated to 375 F for eighteen minutes. Cool before using.

To Assemble Sandwiches:

9.Place two tbsps. butter in a frying pan on a medium flame.

10. Fry 3 eggs until the yolks have just set. Fry the remaining three eggs in a similar manner.

11. Slice the rolls and add three hams slices, the egg and two ounces cheese, then replace the roll top on each sandwich.

12. Place the sandwiches two at a time into the frying pan to which two tablespoons of butter have been added and brown on both sides. Flatten with a spatula as they fry.

13. Cut sandwiches in half and sprinkle with the powdered sugar while still hot.

**Pairs well with** – fries, olives, jalapenos

# 7. Chicken and Root Vegetable Soup

This is a hearty chicken soup and also a Puerto Rican favorite.

Serves 6 to 8

**Ingredients**

2 tablespoons canola oil

3 crushed cloves garlic

1 large minced yellow onion

1 large peeled and cubed green plantain

10 C. chicken stock

Kosher salt and black pepper to taste

3 peeled medium carrots, sliced into rounds

8 cilantro sprigs

8 chicken thighs, skin removed

8 ounces 1" diced red potatoes, peeled

2 ounces spaghetti, each piece broken in two

1 finely chopped plum tomato, seeds and core removed

## Preparation

1. Place the oil in a deep sauce pan to heat up then add the onions, tomatoes and garlic to cook for eight minutes.

2. Pour in the stock, then add the cilantro and chicken, cook for twenty more minutes.

3. Add the potatoes, plantains and carrots, cook for a further twenty-five minutes.

4. Take chicken out and shred, removing the bones and the fat. Place back in pot and now add spaghetti, cook until al dente. Add salt and pepper to taste.


**Pairs well with** – pan de Mallorca

# 8. Ramp Escabeche

Escabeche sauce is a vinegary pickling sauce commonly used as a preservative. In this version the ramps are grilled to increase the flavor and combined with the escabeche sauce. It is common for this sauce to be stored for multiple uses, for at least two months. If kept in a sealed glass jar in the refrigerator, you can enjoy it with meal after meal.

Serves 6 to 8

**Ingredients**

7 ½ ounces trimmed ramps

Coarse ground black pepper

½ C. and 2 tbsps. olive oil

¾ C. rice vinegar

¼ C. honey

Kosher salt

**Preparation**

1. Use two tablespoons of the olive oil to toss the ramps along with some salt and place them on a lit grill.

2. Allow them to char slightly (about two to three minutes) then place them inside a glass jar.

3. Pour the honey and vinegar into a saucepan and simmer on a medium flame.

4. When the mixture has been reduced to two-thirds of its amount, pour the liquid over the ramps in the jar as well as the olive oil, then add salt and pepper.

5. Cover the jar and cool fully before use. Keep in fridge for two months to store.

**Pairs well with** – fish and plantains

# 9. Arroz con Gandules (Puerto Rican Rice with Pigeon Peas)

This rice dish is not your typical rice and peas. It is great for vegetarians who may rely on peas as a source of protein, in which case it can be had on its own. Otherwise it pairs well with various meats and has added surprises in the mix.

Serves 6 to 8

**Ingredients**

3 tablespoons canola oil

2 ounces cubed bacon

1 teaspoon dried oregano

15 ounces drained pigeon peas

2 tablespoons tomato paste

½ C. sofrito

½ minced yellow onion, small

2 C. long-grain rice, white

2 C. chicken stock

3 ½ ounces olive/capers/pimiento mix (from jar)

Salt and fresh black pepper

## Preparation

1. Put the oil to heat in a saucepan and cook the bacon until brown.

2. Add the sofrito and onions then cook until the onions are soft.

3. Next add the rice and tomato paste, then add the stock, olive mixture and oregano. After two minutes, bring to a boil.

4. Turn the heat down to low and cook until the rice is ready.

5. Add the peas, cook for a further ten minutes, add salt and pepper to taste then serve.


**Pairs well with** – roasted pork or pasteles

# 10. Coquito French Toast

This coconut flavored French toast owes its goodness to coquito. Not your average French toast due to the addition of rum, it is sure to add a nice kick to the start of your day or the end!

Serves 4 to 6

**Ingredients**

1 pound loaf of challah bread, 1" thick slices

Maple syrup

2 C. coquito

Ground cinnamon

2 tbsps. unsalted butter (cut into 1/2 inch pieces, plus a little extra for greasing)

Powdered sugar

**Preparation**

1. Preheat the oven to 400 F.

2. Grease a rectangular baking dish (glass or ceramic) then make a single layer with the slices of bread and overlap them slightly.

3. Pour the coquito over the bread and allow them to soak. Turn the slices over and arrange again to allow all the liquid to be absorbed.

4. Distribute the pieces of butter on the surface of the bread then place in the oven. Bake for thirty minutes until puffy and golden brown.

5. Sprinkle with powdered sugar and cinnamon, then add a little maple syrup to serve.


**Pairs well with** – fresh berries

# 11. Smoked Chorizo Surullos

These smoked chorizo surullos are a spin on the regular surullito and can be enjoyed as an appetizer or a snack. They are a Puerto Rican staple.

**Serves 6**

**Ingredients**

½ tbsp avocado oil

2 C. warm water

½ C. smoked chorizo sausage

2 tbsps sugar

Salt and pepper

1½ C. white cornmeal

Vegetable oil, for frying

Red pepper flakes

1tbsp melted butter

## Preparation

1. Heat the oven beforehand to 350 F and use aluminum foil to line a baking tray.

2. Heat the vegetable oil in a deep heavy frying pan and when the oil ripples it is ready for frying.

3. Add the sausage mixed with avocado oil to a light frying pan, cook until chorizo becomes crispy, then place aside for later.

4. Mix the water, salt, sugar and butter together then add the cornmeal a little at a time, to make a batter.

5. Add the sausage and mix in then continue to add the cornmeal to make a dough.

6. Using oiled hands, make about 2" long log-like shapes with the dough about ½ ins in thickness and fry them in small batches. They are ready when golden and crispy.

7. Keep in oven to maintain warmth.

**Pairs well with** – mayo or ketchup

# 12. Pineapple Paraiso Cocktail

This perfect summer cocktail can be had at all times of the year, especially if enjoying in tropical climates. It's the ideal thirst quencher on a hot day with a lovely blend of pineapple, orange and lime juices, with ginger and the right amount of alcohol.

**Serves 2**

**Ingredients**

¼ oz. agave nectar

½ oz. Suze Liqueur

1 ¼ oz Cabrito Blanco

Muddled ginger with sage

¾ oz. lime juice

1 squeezed Cara Cara Orange

4 muddled pineapple chunks

## Preparation

1. Shake all ingredients strenuously using a shaker.

2. Strain twice and serve in a coupe glass over ice.


**Pairs well with** - Mallorcas

# 13. Pastelón

The various components of this meal all come together to make a delicious treat which stands boldly on its own.

Serves 5

**Ingredients**

1small finely chopped onion

2 minced cloves garlic

1/3 C. minced green bell pepper

3 tbsps vegetable oil

2 sprigs cilantro, finely chopped

1/3 tsp annatto powder or paste

1/3 C. green olives, sliced

1 ½ lbs ground beef

½ C. oil for frying

1 ½ tsps salt

¼ tsp black pepper

1 tsp oregano

2 tbsps chopped pimientos

½ tsp cumin

1 tbsp capers

3 lbs extra ripe plantains, skin removed and sliced into thin rounds

2 tbsps raisins

½ C. tomato sauce

2 beaten eggs

1 pack frozen string beans, cut lengthwise (thawed and drained)

## Preparation

1. Sauté the onions, garlic, peppers, cilantro and annatto in a skillet in the oil on a medium flame. Do so for a total of one minute, with constant stirring.

2. Add the ground beef then sauté for a couple of minutes until evenly browned.

3. Add the salt, pepper, cumin and oregano. Stir and cook for one more minute.

4. Add the capers, raisins, olives, pimientos and sauce, cooking for a further two minutes with constant stirring.

5. Take pot off the heat and allow the contents to cool.

6. In a separate pan, heat two cups oil to fry the plantains. They will be slightly brown when done. Drain on absorbent paper.

7. Place the fried plantain at the bottom of a nine inch square baking pan or dish. Ensure the edges somewhat overlap to cover the base well.

8. Brush the plantains with a little beaten egg then place an even layer of the meat on top

9. Add a layer of string beans using up half of the amount, then repeat the plantain layer, meat layer and so forth, until the final layer is a layer of plantains with beaten egg.

10. In an oven preheated to 350 F, bake for twenty-five minutes to half an hour. The surface will turn brown. Cool for twenty minutes then loosen the edges of the casserole with a knife.

11. Turn out onto an inverted serving platter over the mouth of the baking dish then cut into squares.

**Pairs well with** – steamed rice

# 14. Asopao with Shrimp and Vegetables

This soup does not contain root vegetables however it does contain tasty shrimp rice and mixed vegetables, making this Puerto Rican creation a complete meal option or a side dish in a smaller portion size.

**Serves 12**

**Ingredients**

1tbsp annato seeds

36 medium-sized shrimp

½ C. chopped onions

1 tsp dried oregano

6 small minced red Chile peppers, seeds removed

4 minced cloves garlic

8 C. chicken broth

½ C. Olive Oil

2 C. tomato sauce

4 bay leaves

1 tsp salt

32 ozs. frozen mixed vegetables

4 C. cooked white rice

## Preparation

1. Heat the annatto seeds with the oil in a big sauce pan on a medium/high flame.

2. When the oil turns red, strain it into a small container and throw the seeds away.

3. Pour the oil back into the pot and cook the peppers and onions, until the onions are translucent.

4. Toss in garlic and sauté for half a minute then pour in broth, sauce, dried oregano, salt and add the bay leaves.

5. Boil then add the mixed vegetables, turn the heat down to a medium flame then cook for roughly seven minutes.

6. Put in the shrimp and rice then cover and turn off when the shrimp turns pink, typically after five minutes or so.


**Pairs well with** – pan de Mallorca

# 15. Piragua de Crema de Mango con Vainilla (Mango Cream Shaved Ice with Vanilla)

This rich and extra creamy mango vanilla shaved ice is a winner and meets all the expectations of a tropical delight. It is refreshing and if you want to jazz it up a little more you may choose to add a splash of rum.

**Serves 4**

**Ingredients**

1lb peeled ripe mangoes, seeds removed

7 ½ C. shaved ice

11 ounces evaporated milk

1tsp vanilla extract

13 ounces condensed milk

**Preparation**

1. Puree the mango, condensed and evaporated milk with the vanilla until smooth.

2. Split the ice evenly between four long glasses then pour in the mango puree and enjoy.


**Pairs well with** – white chocolate cake

# 16. Mofongo

This Puerto Rican staple is an interesting fried mashed plantain which serves as a side dish for many entrees.

Serves 4

## Ingredients

4 green plantains

2 cup olive oil (canola oil)

Salt to taste

6 cloves garlic

2 tbsp extra virgin olive oil

1 lb crispy fried pork rinds

1 slice cooked bacon

8 oz chicken stock (low sodium)

## Preparation

1. Peel then slice the plantains into 1" rounds.
2. Fry the plantains in very hot oil for a total of seven minutes, both sides. Drain excess oil using paper towels.
3. Using a large pestle and mortar, crush the garlic with salt then add olive oil pounding well. Place in a small dish.
4. Crush half the plantains in the mortar along with half the pork rinds, half the bacon and half of the previously crushed garlic.
5. Add half of the chicken stock if necessary, to moisten.
6. Make 2" balls from the mash and keep warm until serving time.
7. Remember to mash the remaining half of the fried plantains in a similar manner.

**Pairs well with** – salad or rice and beans

# 17. Chicken Asopao

This hearty one dish meal is a traditional Puerto Rican fixing. It is chock full of flavor with chicken, olives, garlic, onions, rice and pepper flakes. It is a very thick stew and goes wonderfully with avocado slices.

Serves 6

**Ingredients**

2 lb chicken thighs (bones and skins removed)

½ tsp black pepper

1 adobo seasoning sachet

3 tbsp olive oil

1 diced green bell pepper

1 diced medium onion

4 minced garlic gloves

2 tbsp tomato paste

1 ½ cup rice

14 ½ oz diced canned tomatoes

6 cup chicken broth (low sodium)

1 bay leaf

¼ tsp red pepper flakes

1 cup petite peas (frozen kind but thawed)

1 cup sliced green olives (with pimentos)

¼ cup fresh cilantro (chopped)

## Preparation

1. Use the adobo seasoning and black pepper to rub the chicken well.
2. Cook the peppers, onions, garlic and tomato paste in hot oil then put aside.
3. Brown the thighs on either side by frying then add the cooked vegetables, rice, tomatoes, broth, bay leaf, and pepper flakes.
4. Allow to boil then lower flame to allow contents to simmer for twenty minutes.
5. Add the peas and sliced olives then continue cooking for five more minutes. Turn flame off and remove bay leaf.
6. Add in the cilantro then serve.

**Pairs well with** – sliced avocado, cilantro

# 18. Puerto Rican Roasted Pork

This well-flavored pork shoulder is also called Pernil. In other parts of the region it is served as a special occasion meal typically at Christmas and New Year. The leftovers are used to make sandwiches.

Serves 8

**Ingredients**

2 oz olive oil

3 tbsp vinegar

10 garlic cloves (or more)

2 tbsp oregano flakes

1 tbsp salt

1 ½ tsps black pepper

5 lb pork shoulder (extra fat removed)

## Preparation

1. Meld all the ingredients except the pork together in a mortar and pestle.
2. Making slits into the pork using a knife, push the paste down into the holes then rub the remainder all over the meat.
3. Put the pork inside a plastic roasting bag, rest in roasting pan with rack and marinate in fridge for between 8 hours and 2 days.
4. Bring the pork to room temperature before serving. Perhaps for an hour or two.
5. Set the oven to 300 °F or 150 °C.
6. Rest the pork on the side with the skin on the rack in the roasting pan for two hours. It will become golden brown.
7. Turn on the other side and roast until the juices run clear, in about two to four hours. An internal thermometer should read about 145 °F or 63 C when it is ready.

**Pairs well with** – salad, rice and beans, sweet plantains

# 19. Arroz con Pollo

This highly aromatic rice and chicken meal is quite simple to prepare and is quite flavorful. It is much more than a simple rice with chicken dish. It is a beautiful saffron color which makes it even more appealing to the senses and pleasing to the eyes.

Serves 4

## Ingredients

3 cup rinsed rice

2 lb chicken parts (skin removed)

4 ½ oz tomato sauce

2 tbsp alcaparrado

Salt

½ tsp black pepper

2 tbsp Sofrito

2 tbsp vegetable oil

4 cup of boiling water

1 sazon with saffron sachet

## Preparation

1. In a very big dutch oven, brown the pieces of chicken for five minutes on either side, using the oil.
2. Set the chicken aside once finished and add the other ingredients but not the rice and water to the drippings.
3. Mix them well cooking the sofrito for at least five minutes. Taste for salt.
4. Now add the browned chicken as well as the rice and mix.
5. Add the hot water to an inch above the level of the rice and mix.
6. Cook with the pot open and all the water dries off.
7. Use a wooden spoon to stir the contents from bottom to top then put lid on and cook on a low flame for about 20 or 25 minutes for the rice to become tender.

**Pairs well with** – green beans, steamed vegetables

# Conclusion

After having tried some of these recipes, you will most certainly crave more. Puerto Rico has so much to offer for your culinary pleasure. It is a country with a rich history, as does much of the Caribbean. If you have never been, then Puerto Rico is the place to visit for wonderful tastes and aromas however until your visit, simply bring Puerto Rico into your kitchen, with these fantastic recipes!

If you have a craving for more Caribbean recipes then be sure to check out my other books and gain further skills to add to your repertoire:

Just a reminder…don't forget to visit **www.ffdrecipes.com** for your FREE bonus cookbooks and to get exclusive access to our World Recipes Club, which provides FREE book offers, discounts and recipe ideas!

Thank you.

# Cooking Measurements & Conversions

## Oven Temperature Conversions

Use the below table as a guide to establishing the correct temperatures when cooking, however please be aware that oven types and models and location of your kitchen can have an influence on temperature also.

| °F | °C | Gas Mark | Explanation |
|---|---|---|---|
| 275°F | 140°C | 1 | cool |
| 300°F | 150°C | 2 | |
| 325°F | 170°C | 3 | very moderate |
| 350°F | 180°C | 4 | moderate |
| 375°F | 190°C | 5 | |
| 400°F | 200°C | 6 | moderately hot |
| 425°F | 220°C | 7 | hot |
| 450°F | 230°C | 8 | |
| 475°F | 240°C | 9 | very hot |

# US to Metric Corresponding Measures

| Metric | Imperial |
|---|---|
| 3 teaspoons | 1 tablespoon |
| 1 tablespoon | 1/16 cup |
| 2 tablespoons | 1/8 cup |
| 2 tablespoons + 2 teaspoons | 1/6 cup |
| 4 tablespoons | 1/4 cup |
| 5 tablespoons + 1 teaspoon | 1/3 cup |
| 6 tablespoons | 3/8 cup |
| 8 tablespoons | 1/2 cup |
| 10 tablespoons + 2 teaspoons | 2/3 cup |
| 12 tablespoons | 3/4 cup |
| 16 tablespoons | 1 cup |
| 48 teaspoons | 1 cup |

| | |
|---|---|
| 8 fluid ounces (fl oz) | 1 cup |
| 1 pint | 2 cups |
| 1 quart | 2 pints |
| 1 quart | 4 cups |
| 1 gallon (gal) | 4 quarts |
| 1 cubic centimeter (cc) | 1 milliliter (ml) |
| 2.54 centimeters (cm) | 1 inch (in) |
| 1 pound (lb) | 16 ounces (oz) |

# Liquid to Volume

| Metric | Imperial |
| --- | --- |
| 15ml | 1 tbsp |
| 55 ml | 2 fl oz |
| 75 ml | 3 fl oz |
| 150 ml | 5 fl oz (¼ pint) |
| 275 ml | 10 fl oz (½ pint) |
| 570 ml | 1 pint |
| 725 ml | 1 ¼ pints |
| 1 litre | 1 ¾ pints |
| 1.2 litres | 2 pints |
| 1.5 litres | 2½ pints |
| 2.25 litres | 4 pints |

# Weight Conversion

| Metric | Imperial |
|--------|----------|
| 10 g | ½ oz |
| 20 g | ¾ oz |
| 25 g | 1 oz |
| 40 g | 1½ oz |
| 50 g | 2 oz |
| 60 g | 2½ oz |
| 75 g | 3 oz |
| 110 g | 4 oz |
| 125 g | 4½ oz |
| 150 g | 5 oz |
| 175 g | 6 oz |
| 200 g | 7 oz |
| 225 g | 8 oz |
| 250 g | 9 oz |
| 275 g | 10 oz |

| | |
|---|---|
| 350 g | 12 oz |
| 450 g | 1 lb |
| 700 g | 1 lb 8 oz |
| 900 g | 2 lb |
| 1.35 kg | 3 lb |

# Cooking Abbreviations

| Abbreviation | Description |
|:---:|:---:|
| tsp | teaspoon |
| Tbsp | tablespoon |
| c | cup |
| pt | pint |
| qt | quart |
| gal | gallon |
| wt | weight |
| oz | ounce |
| lb | pound |
| g | gram |
| kg | kilogram |
| vol | volume |
| ml | milliliter |
| fl oz | fluid ounce |

# Special Request...

As you can tell, I'm passionate about Caribbean food and eager to share this wonderful cuisine with as many people as I can. If you don't mind, I'd like to ask you for your help to enable more people to discover the food we love.

I'm seeking feedback from readers and I would greatly appreciate it if you would leave a review. I really value your opinion!

Again, I really appreciate you taking the time to read the book and provide feedback!

Thank you very much.

Made in the USA
Middletown, DE
30 November 2019

79673506R00031